★ ★ ★ IT'S MY STATE! ★ ★ ★

WASHINGTON

Steven Otfinoski

Tea Benduhn

 **Marshall Cavendish**
Benchmark
New York

Other Marshall Cavendish Offices:
Marshall Cavendish International (Asia) Private Limited, 1 New Industrial Road, Singapore 536196 •
Marshall Cavendish International (Thailand) Co Ltd. 253 Asoke, 12th Flr, Sukhumvit 21 Road, Klongtoey Nua, Wattana, Bangkok 10110, Thailand • Marshall Cavendish (Malaysia) Sdn Bhd, Times Subang, Lot 46, Subang Hi-Tech Industrial Park, Batu Tiga, 40000 Shah Alam, Selangor Darul Ehsan, Malaysia

Marshall Cavendish is a trademark of Times Publishing Limited

All websites were available and accurate when this book was sent to press.

Library of Congress Cataloging-in-Publication Data
Otfinoski, Steven.
        Washington / Steven Otfinoski and Tea Benduhn. — 2nd ed.
            p. cm. — (It's my state!)
        Includes index.
        ISBN 978-1-60870-061-5
        1. Washington (State)—Juvenile literature. I. Benduhn, Tea. II. Title.
    F891.3.O84 2011
    979.7—dc22   2010003935

Second Edition developed for Marshall Cavendish Benchmark by RJF Publishing LLC (www.RJFpublishing.com)
Series Designer, Second Edition: Tammy West/Westgraphix LLC
Editor, Second Edition: Amanda Hudson

All maps, illustrations, and graphics © Marshall Cavendish Corporation. Maps and artwork on pages 6, 44, 45, 75, and back cover by Christopher Santoro. Map and graphics on pages 8 and 40 by Westgraphix LLC. Map on page 76 by Mapping Specialists.

The photographs in this book are used by permission and through the courtesy of:
Front cover: neelsky & Orange Line Media (inset)/Shutterstock.
Alamy: All Canada Photos, 4 (bottom); North Wind Picture Archives, 27; Big Cheese Photo LLC, 38; Danita Delimont, 42, 54; Tim Laman/National Geographic Image Collection, 51; Daniel Beams, 53; imac, 56; Greg Vaughn, 59; Edmund Lowe, 67; Visions of America, LLC, 68; Aurora Photos, 71 (bottom); Corbis Premium RF, 74. **AP Images:** John Froschauer, 61. **Corbis:** Jim Cummins, 46. **Getty Images:** Altrendo Nature, 4 (top); Scientifica/Visuals Unlimited, 5; Panoramic Images, 9; Art Wolfe, 10; Bob Stefko, 11; John Marshall, 12; Erik Hovmiller Photography, 13; Walter Bibikow, 14; Steve Satushek, 15; Wolfgang Bayer/Discovery Channel Images, 16; William Weber/Visuals Unlimited, 17 (top); Fred Felleman, 17 (bottom); Chip Porter, 18; Bruce Forster, 20 (top); Roy Toft/National Geographic, 20 (bottom); Jeff Foott/Discovery Channel Images, 21; Margaret Bourke-White/Time & Life Pictures, 34; Dorothea Lange/Hulton Archive, 35; A. Dawburne/Stringer/Hulton Archive, 36; Buyenlarge/Hulton Archive, 41 (top); David Hiser, 41 (bottom); Chris Cheadle, 48; Clive Brunskill 49, (left); Timothy A. Clary/AFP, 49 (right); Terrence Vaccaro/National Basketball Association, 50; Karen Moskowitz, 62; Fry Design Ltd, 65; Rich Frishman, 66; Kevin Horan, 69; Scott Barbour/Stringer, 70; Bloomberg, 71 (top); Jeremy Woodhouse , 72. **Northwest Museum of Arts & Culture/Eastern Washington State Historical Society, Spokane, Washington:** L96-2.127, Thomas W. Tolman, 24. **Office of the Governor, Washington:** 47. **Philip Palermo:** 55. USDA: 64. **U.S. Fish and Wildlife Service:** 19. **University of Washington Libraries, Special Collections:** CKK0596, 22; UW 2113, 30; CUR 706, 31; UW 24311z, 32. **Washington State Historical Society:** 25, 26.

Printed in Malaysia (T).
135642

CONTENTS

A Quick Look at
WASHINGTON

State Flower: Coast Rhododendron

The name rhododendron means "rose tree." The plant's beautiful flowers grow in clusters. Rhododendrons have large shiny evergreen leaves that are poisonous when eaten. The coast rhododendron was chosen as Washington's state flower in 1892.

State Bird: Willow Goldfinch

The goldfinch is a small bird with yellow markings and black wings. It is sometimes called the wild canary because of its sweet song. The goldfinch's cup-shaped nest can hold water because it is built so tightly.

State Tree: Western Hemlock

The western hemlock is a type of pine tree that can grow to be as tall as 200 feet (60 meters). Washington's early residents used the tree's reddish-brown bark for tanning leather and dyeing objects. The wood was also used to carve eating and cooking utensils and other tools.

State Gem: Petrified Wood

Petrified wood was created millions of years ago in Washington's swampy interior. Water seeped into the trees, and substances in the water—such as silica—gradually replaced the wood. Eventually, these substances hardened, and the wood turned to stone or a stonelike material. Petrified wood often has the same shape as the original wood.

State Fish: Steelhead Trout

Washington's state fish can be silver-gray with spots along its back. Some of these trout may have pinkish red colorings, and others have white bellies. Steelhead trout are born in fresh water but migrate—or move—to the salt waters of the ocean. As adults, the fish return to freshwater streams and rivers to breed the next generation of fish.

State Dance: Square Dance

The square dance became Washington's official dance in 1979. The square dance is a type of folk dance brought to the West by settlers and pioneers. Square dancing is very popular among many of the state's residents—Washington even offers an official license plate designed for people who are very enthusiastic about the dance.

The Evergreen State

Washington is the only state in the nation named for a president: George Washington. Because the nation's capital is called Washington, D.C., the state is often called Washington State to avoid confusion. Like the first president, Washington is first in many things, such as the production of apples and sweet cherries and the manufacturing of airplanes and other technology products.

Washington is located in the northwestern corner of the contiguous, or connected, forty-eight U.S. states. The state's northern, eastern, and southeastern borders are fairly straight (generally following lines of latitude or longitude, except where the Snake River makes up the southernmost part of the eastern border). The southwestern border, which follows the Columbia River, is much more irregular in shape, as is the western border, which is the coast of the Pacific Ocean. On a map, Washington looks like something took a bite out of its northwestern corner, where the large inlet called Puget Sound is located. Washington is the smallest of the three contiguous states bordering the Pacific Ocean (the others are Oregon and California). Containing thirty-nine counties, the state has a land area of

Quick Facts

WASHINGTON BORDERS

North	Canada
South	Oregon
East	Idaho
West	Pacific Ocean

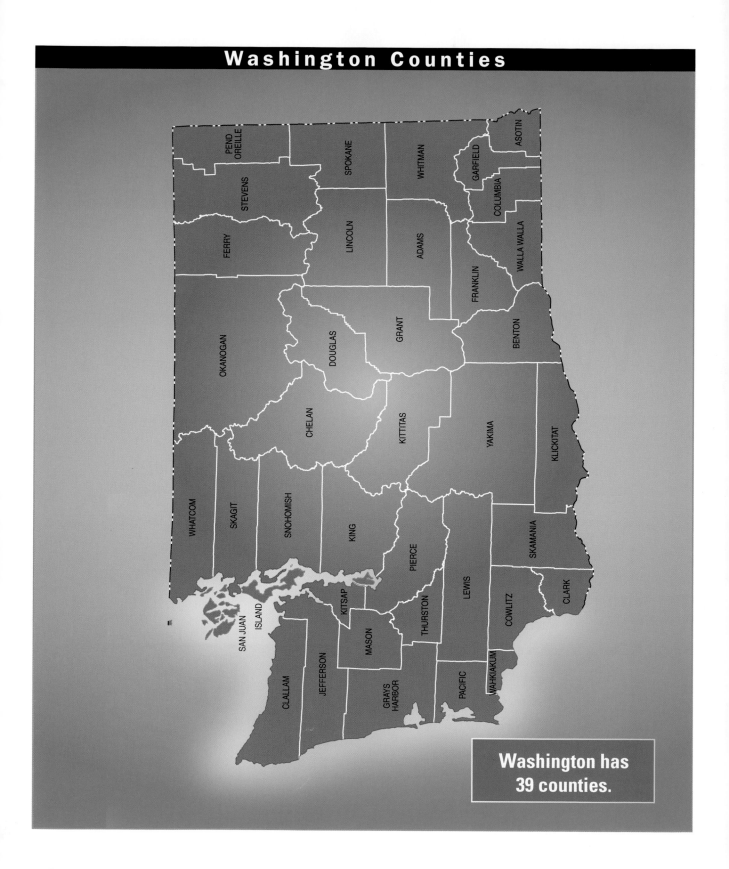

Washington has
39 counties.

66,544 square miles (172,348 square kilometers), making it the twentieth-largest state in the country in land area.

The Landscape

Washington's mountains, valleys, and waterways were formed over the course of millions of years. Glaciers, or slow-moving ice masses, created some of the land features. Volcanic eruptions and land erosion—caused by wind and water—are other factors that altered the surface of the land. The shape and surface of the land have also been affected by the movement of large slabs of rock found beneath Earth's surface. These slabs are called tectonic plates. They move slowly over a very

This beautiful waterfall is part of Palouse Falls State Park, in the eastern part of the state.

RAIN FORESTS

The rain forests of the northwestern United States—called temperate rain forests—are not the same as the humid tropical rain forests found in warm areas such as parts of South America, Asia, and Africa. Mount Olympus, for example, is in a temperate rain forest, and it gets about 100 feet (30 m) of snow each year.

long period of time and can change the appearance of the land above, sometimes creating mountains. The movement of plates also causes earthquakes and volcanic eruptions.

Three major mountain ranges cross through Washington. The Rocky Mountains extend from Canada down to northern New Mexico. A portion of the Rockies stretches across the northeastern corner of Washington. This portion is sometimes called the Selkirk Mountains. The types of animals and plants that live in some parts of the Rockies, such as at high elevations, are very different from the types that live in other areas.

Mount Rainier is Washington's tallest mountain peak.

The Olympic Mountains are located in the northwestern section of the state. These coastal mountains cover approximately 3,500 square miles (9,000 sq km). The highest peak in this mountain range is Mount Olympus, which is about 7,965 feet (2,428 m) high. A large part of the range is located in Olympic National Park. Besides the mountains, the park has rain forests. Rain and fertile soil make the area perfect for trees such as spruce, hemlock, cedars, and firs, as well as for other plants, including moss. Elk, bears, deer, and mountain lions roam parts of the park.

The Cascade Range is found between the Rockies and the Olympic Mountains. The mountains of the Cascades run from north to south and divide the state almost in half. The Cascades contain Mount Rainier, the tallest peak in the state at 14,410 feet (4,392 m). Mount Rainier is actually a volcano, although it has not erupted since 1882.

The same cannot be said of Mount Saint Helens, which is farther south in the Cascades. In 1980, Mount Saint Helens erupted, blowing its top. The volcano lost more than 1,300 feet (400 m) of its top, opening a crater, and went from being the fifth highest peak in the state to the thirteenth. It was the first volcanic eruption in any state except for Alaska or Hawaii in nearly sixty years. Hot ash rained down, ruining crops and destroying wildlife. The tremendous heat caused the surrounding snow to melt. The melted snow caused flooding and mud slides.

Mount Saint Helens is a volcano located in the Cascade mountain range.

The volcanic explosions were so strong that they knocked down hundreds of acres of trees. The eruption caused billions of dollars in damage, and more than fifty people died.

Since the eruption, wildlife has flourished again, and communities have been rebuilt. Mount Saint Helens erupted again in 2004, but the new eruption was not as destructive. Lava pierced the crater floor, and the volcano erupted continually until 2008, building a new lava dome.

Volcanic eruptions that occurred thousands of years ago helped to create the region east of the Cascades, called the Columbia Plateau. A plateau is land that is flat on top but is located at a high elevation. The Columbia Plateau is raised up because of hardened lava that flowed from the volcanic eruptions. Cities such as Spokane, Walla Walla, and Yakima are located on the plateau. The Yakima, Columbia, and Spokane rivers flow through the area, and the land around those rivers tends to be fertile and ideal for growing crops, such as wheat.

Washington Waterways

Washington has many bodies of water flowing into, out of, and across the state. A long arm of water called the Strait of Juan de Fuca leads from the Pacific Ocean into Puget Sound. The sound was created thousands of years ago when glaciers moved through the area and carved up the land. Most of the state's population lives in the area around Puget Sound. Three of the state's major cities—Seattle, Tacoma, and the capital, Olympia—are near the sound.

Puget Sound is also home to many islands. Bainbridge Island is just a ferry ride away from Seattle. The San Juan Islands attract visitors who enjoy activities such as hiking, sailing, scuba diving, and exploring the state parks. Residents of the islands create their own thriving communities.

The Columbia River flows through the Columbia Plateau.

The state also has many rivers, streams, and lakes. The Puyallup River flows past Tacoma into Puget Sound. Other rivers, such as the Quinault, flow into the Pacific Ocean.

The longest river in Washington is the Columbia. It begins in British Columbia, a province of Canada, and cuts down through the middle of Washington. At the bottom of the state, the river heads westward and forms much of the border between Washington and Oregon.

The Columbia River empties into the Pacific Ocean at Cape Disappointment. The Snake River, Lewis River, Spokane River, Klickitat River, and Cowlitz River are just some of the rivers that flow into the Columbia River. The Columbia carries with it more than half of the water that falls as precipitation in the state. Washington has harnessed the power of the Columbia River with human-made dams that control flooding and create electricity, and water from the reservoirs that form behind the dams is used to irrigate farmland. The damming, however, has caused controversy. The dams were built to control the river, but as a result, other areas were permanently flooded when the reservoirs were created. Animal habitats and wildlife were destroyed. The dams also affect the migration of some types of fish, especially salmon.

There are more than one thousand natural lakes in Washington. The largest natural lake is Lake Chelan, located in the central region. The state has larger lakes, but they are artificial—reservoirs created by dams. Lake Roosevelt, the largest such lake, is more than 150 miles (240 km) long. It was named for President Franklin D. Roosevelt. A national recreation area was created next to the lake, giving visitors and residents the opportunity to swim, fish, hike, and camp.

Climate

Thanks to the moist air blowing in from the Pacific Ocean, Washington's western coast has mild winters and cool summers. No other part of the United States that far north has such warm winter weather. The ocean winds also contain lots of moisture that turns into rain. Western Washington is one of the wettest places in the nation. The region gets rain an average of 150 to 180 days a year and has areas of rain forest. All that rain is good for trees and plants. The region also gets some snow in the wintertime. As expected, more snow falls at the higher elevations. Mount Baker, which is near Bellingham, holds the record for the heaviest winter snowfall in the country. In 1999, an amazing 95 feet (29 m) of snow fell.

Mount Baker gets a lot of snow in the winter. In warmer months, it is full of wildflowers.

In Their Own Words

To live in Washington is always to be aware that wilderness is just outside the door, partly because it's just inside the door as well. . . . We enter the indoors with the rain in our clothes.
—Carrie Brownstein, a Washington resident

The Cascade Range tends to block the warm and moist Pacific air from reaching eastern Washington, giving that part of the state a different climate. The winters are usually very cold and the summers are hot. The temperatures can go well below 0 degrees Fahrenheit (-18 degrees Celsius) in the winter and above 100 °F (38 °C) in the summer. Rainfall is not as heavy in this part of the state. Some parts of the eastern region average only about 6 inches (15 centimeters) of rain each year.

Life in the Wild

Washington's thick forests are home to tall Douglas fir, Sitka spruce, and western hemlock, the state tree. Some of the trees are hundreds of years old. Cottonwood, maple, and ash trees dot the state's lush green forests. Lodgepole pines and western larch grow tall in the less-wooded eastern region. Warm areas of the state have different types of mosses and ferns.

Wildflowers thrive in the mild, wet climate of Puget Sound. Fields and meadows are bright with brown- and black-eyed Susans, lupine, goldenrod, and Indian paintbrush. Coast rhododendron, the state flower, covers hillsides and slopes in the Cascades' foothills.

Quick Facts

MOUNTAIN LIONS
Mountain lions are the largest cat in Washington. They are about 7 feet (2 m) long and can weigh 200 pounds (90 kilograms). They can leap 30 feet (9 m) forward from a standstill and 20 feet (6 m) straight up a cliff wall. About 2,500 mountain lions live in the wilderness, but they are rarely seen.

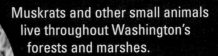
Muskrats and other small animals live throughout Washington's forests and marshes.

Washington's forests and marshes are filled with small animals. These include beavers, minks, muskrats, and marmots. Larger animals, such as mountain lions, mountain goats, and coyotes, can also be found in different parts of the state. Many types of deer call Washington home. They include the elk and the mule deer.

Throughout the state, lakes and rivers are filled with whitefish, giant sturgeon, and several kinds of trout. The offshore waters of the Pacific swarm with seals, porpoises, salmon, and some of the largest octopuses found anywhere in the world. Whales such as orcas and gray whales can be seen traveling along the coast.

Bald eagles and cranes are just two of the birds that can be found in the state. Flocks of pelicans, puffins, seagulls, and oystercatchers fly above the state's waters. Washington's temperate rain forests also have spotted owls, flycatchers, and crossbills.

Orcas, or killer whales, can be found along the coast of Washington.

Protecting the Environment

As Washington's population grew over the past century, more towns and cities were developed, and the wilderness began to disappear. The logging industry has been responsible for clearing away forests and other wilderness. Logging has long been an important and profitable industry for Washington. The industry provides money for the state and keeps many Washington residents employed. But the land has been harmed by all the years of cutting down trees. Bare patches of land that were once filled with trees and plants can now be found throughout the state. Efforts to replant trees have been made, but it is impossible to replace all the cut trees. Logging has also destroyed many habitats of woodland creatures and wild plants.

The logging industry keeps many Washingtonians employed, but cutting down so many trees has harmed the land.

The woodland caribou is an endangered animal.

Forests filled with different trees, plants, and animals were also cleared to make space for homes, factories, and roads. Rivers were dammed, interfering with migration and growth of different types of fish, such as salmon. Many animals lost their homes and their food, and soon their populations started to decrease. When a type of animal is in danger of disappearing, it is listed as endangered. This means that it is illegal to hunt the animal or to interfere with its habitat. Many Washingtonians work hard to protect these endangered animals.

The woodland caribou is one example of an endangered animal. These large animals are actually wild reindeer. They once roamed freely across nine northern states. Now their only populations in the United States are found in the Selkirk Mountains of Washington and Idaho. To study and replenish the number of caribou, the U.S. Fish and Wildlife Service and scientists in British Columbia, Canada, started a special project. Scientists fly in helicopters and airplanes above places where the caribou live. They count the number of caribou tracks, or hoof prints, and the number of animals they see every year. They also use rifles that fire a special net to briefly capture caribou. They mark or tag the animals and then release them in the Selkirk Mountains. Scientists use the markers or tags to keep track of the individual animals. They follow the animals' movements and learn how they survive.

Plants & Animals

Douglas Fir

This tall evergreen tree can grow as high as 250 feet (76 m). The tallest one, found near Little Rock, was 330 feet (100 m) tall. The average life span of a Douglas fir is 500 years, though it can live for up to 1,000. The oldest one, found near Mount Vernon, was 1,400 years old when it was cut down.

Lupine

A member of the pea family, the lupine plant has clusters of colorful flowers. Lupine can be pink, blue, white, or a mixture of these colors. There are around one hundred kinds of lupine in the United States and Canada.

Oystercatcher

This black bird gets its name from its favorite food—oysters. It lives on the shore and uses its long, red-orange bill to pry open the shells of oysters. Oystercatchers lay their eggs on the rocks on the shore.

Orca

Also known as the killer whale, the orca is around 30 feet (9 m) long. Orcas often hunt in packs and prey upon fish, seals, and even other whales. Scientists study these creatures in the open sea and in coastal waters.

Harbor Seal

Puget Sound is home to many harbor seals. These spotted seals enjoy basking on the large rocks and beaches along the sound. Harbor seals may grow to be 7 feet (2 m) long and can weigh more than 200 pounds (90 kg). Their diet includes marine life such as fish and squid.

Mule Deer

The mule deer got its name from its long, furry ears, which resemble those of a mule. It is also known for the unusually stiff way it walks. Its diet consists of grass and the twigs, leaves, and buds of shrubs.

From the Beginning

Present-day Washington was once, in the words of one visitor, a "remote and savage" land. It was one of the last regions of the forty-eight contiguous states to be thoroughly explored. Once people saw the riches of this wilderness, however, growth was rapid. The population has been growing ever since.

Native Peoples

The first inhabitants of present-day Washington were American Indians. They arrived there at least 12,000 years ago. At that time a frozen land bridge connected North America with Asia. People from Asia crossed over the land bridge and eventually spread out and settled in different parts of North America.

By the time European explorers first arrived, there were many tribes living in Washington. They were divided into two main groups. Those that lived west of the Cascades included the Chinook, Clatsop, Nooksack, and Puyallup. These people lived in permanent homes made of red cedar wood. They fished for salmon in rivers and along the coast and hunted deer in the green forests.

The people east of the Cascades lived very different lives. They included the Cayuse, Yakama, Colville, and Nez Perce. Their land was dry because it received little rain. Their way of life often followed the seasons. They gathered roots, berries, and other plants but also fished and hunted deer and other animals. Some American Indians would move from place to place, following the animals

These children attended school at a logging camp in the 1920s. Logging is an important part of Washington's history.

This group of tepees belonged to the Colville, one of the American Indian tribes that lived east of the Cascades.

they were hunting. The Nez Perce, for example, moved their homes to different locations depending upon the seasons. During certain parts of the year, they set up temporary camps near areas where they could collect plants, berries, and roots. At other times, they lived near the rivers to fish and hunt animals. Many Nez Perce lived in longhouses. These mat-covered structures could fit several families. The Nez Perce also used tipis made of wooden poles and covered with animal skins.

For thousands of years, American Indians in this region developed thriving communities. They had their own belief systems, languages, and customs. But American Indian life began to change as explorers from Europe and other parts of North America traveled to the area.

The First Explorers

For two hundred years, explorers traveled to what is now Washington only from the sea. Greek explorer Juan de Fuca claimed to have sailed along the region's shore in 1592. The Strait of Juan de Fuca, leading into Puget Sound, is named for him. British captain George Vancouver retraced his route two hundred years later and sailed into Puget Sound. He and his men explored the islands of the sound. That same year, American captain Robert Gray sailed into the mouth of the Columbia River. He sailed up the river and named it after his ship, the Columbia. Both the British and the Americans claimed the region.

In November 1805, the American explorers Meriwether Lewis and William Clark reached the Pacific Ocean at the mouth of the Columbia River. They had traveled all the way from St. Louis to explore the Louisiana Purchase (a huge territory between the Mississippi River and the Rocky Mountains that the United States had bought from France in 1803) and to find a water route to the Pacific Ocean. During their travels, they made contact with American Indians who aided them in their journey. Lewis and Clark's celebrated expedition strengthened the United States' claim to the Pacific Northwest.

In Their Own Words

Great joy in camp, we are in view of the [ocean], this Great Pacific Ocean which we [have] been so . . . anxious to see . . .

—explorer William Clark

This illustration imagines Lewis and Clark's famous expedition.

American, Canadian, and British traders soon arrived in the region. They wanted to trade with the American Indians. One of the main items these traders wanted was furs. Hats and other goods made out of fur and leather were popular at the time. Many American Indians traded these animal skins for tools, knives, and other American or British goods.

During the early 1800s, American John Jacob Astor established different sites—or outposts—for fur trading. The outposts around the Columbia River Valley were part of his Pacific Fur Company. In 1811, an outpost named Fort Okanogan was established at the junction of the Okanogan and Columbia rivers. Today, Fort Okanogan State Park overlooks the site of the fort. The park includes a museum with exhibits about the fur-trading industry.

Fort Okanogan, shown here in 1853, was part of John Jacob Astor's Pacific Fur Company.

In 1818, the United States and Great Britain agreed to share the region they called the Oregon Country. This area included the present-day states of Oregon, Washington and Idaho, parts of present-day Montana and Wyoming, and much of the present-day Canadian province of British Columbia. In 1824, Fort Vancouver was established by a British trader named John McLoughlin. Located on the Columbia River, it became the biggest and most important community in what is now Washington.

Missionaries and Pioneers

Some people came to Washington not to make money but to "save souls." In 1836, missionary Marcus Whitman and his wife, Narcissa, set up a mission near Walla Walla. They wanted the American Indians to convert to Christianity.

Soon many American settlers moved west along the Oregon Trail. Americans wanted all of the Oregon Country, and the dispute with Britain over control of the region became more heated. In 1846, the United States

As American settlers moved into Washington, they set up frontier towns.

and Britain reached an agreement. In this agreement, the British gave up their claims to the land south of what was known as the 49th parallel (the imaginary line that represents 49 degrees north latitude). This line became the northern border of Washington. In return, the United States gave up its claims to the land north of the parallel.

American settlers continued to come into the territory. But the American Indians did not want to give up their land. Some of them blamed the missionaries for bringing the settlers west. They also blamed the missionaries for bringing an epidemic of measles that killed many Cayuse children. A group of Cayuse led by Chief Tiloukaikt attacked the Walla Walla mission in 1847. They killed the Whitman family and eleven other people. This attack led to the Cayuse War. American soldiers soon defeated the Indians. Chief Tiloukaikt and the other warriors who had killed the Whitman party voluntarily surrendered. The chief and his warriors were hanged.

Washington Territory

The Oregon Territory was established by an act of Congress in 1848. It included all of present-day Oregon, Washington, and Idaho, as well as parts of Montana and Wyoming. More than one thousand settlers lived in the Washington region in 1850. By 1853, the population had expanded to nearly four thousand. These residents wanted their own territory, so a new act of Congress that year split off the region from the Oregon Territory and created the separate Washington Territory. The residents wanted to name the new territory Columbia, but the government decided to name it Washington, in honor of the first president.

The Washington Territory grew quickly. Part of this growth was a result of the success of the logging camps in the area. Two years before Washington became its own territory, the village of Seattle had been established near Puget Sound.

Chief Seattle of the Duwamish and Suquamish tribes was a friend to the settlers. But other native people felt threatened by them. The territory's governor, Isaac I. Stevens, met with tribal chiefs in 1855 to negotiate treaties. He proposed to buy Indian land in exchange for gifts and money. Many American Indian leaders did not want to give up their land. In an attempt to save their land, these tribes went to war. By 1858, after three years of fighting, the U.S. Army had defeated the Indians. The U.S. government moved many American Indians from their homelands and forced them to live on reservations.

> ## In Their Own Words
>
> *Every part of this soil is sacred in the estimation of my people. Every hillside, every valley, every plain and grove, has been hallowed by some sad or happy event in days long vanished.*
>
> —Chief Seattle

Statehood

The settling of Washington by people from other parts of the United States was slow during the 1860s and 1870s. However, immigrants from other countries began to arrive at this time. Many Chinese immigrants came to the Washington area to prospect for gold, to work on building railroads, or to work in other businesses in the cities. American settlement again increased with the completion of railroad lines in the 1880s. People and goods could now get to the territory quickly and easily. In just ten years, between 1880 and 1890, the territory's population quadrupled. Americans from the East were moving to Washington. As a result of this growth in population, Washington officially became the forty-second state on November 11, 1889.

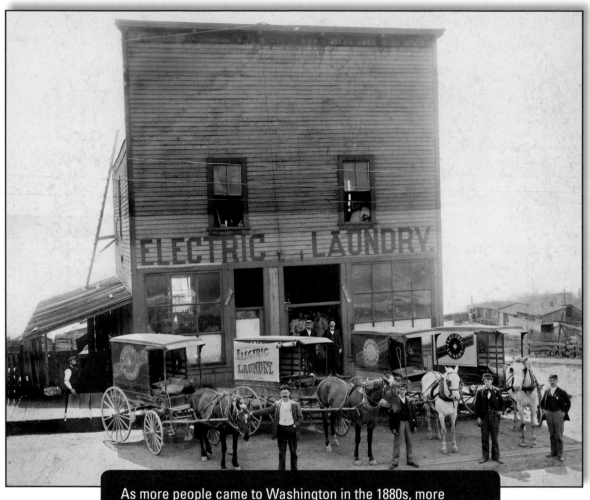

As more people came to Washington in the 1880s, more businesses were created. This photo shows a laundry service.

A Time of Growth

A series of gold rushes helped bring prosperity and more people to Washington. Gold was not discovered in the state, but in the late 1890s, many found riches in the Klondike region, which is located near Alaska in Canada. Thousands of prospectors heading for the gold fields of the Klondike were arriving in Seattle. Almost overnight, Seattle's population exploded. After stopping in Seattle, most prospectors moved north toward the gold. But many stayed in Washington, impressed by its great scenic beauty and economic opportunities.

Industry and farming developed quickly in the early 1900s. Fishing became an important industry in the Puget Sound area. Apple orchards appeared across eastern Washington thanks to new irrigation systems that diverted water to fields used to grow crops. The timber industry became the biggest employer in the state. Shipbuilding also became an important industry. In 1904, the battleship USS *Nebraska* was launched from Moran Brothers shipyard in Seattle.

In 1909, Seattle held a huge fair that was called the Alaska-Yukon-Pacific Exposition. The fair included carnival rides and other forms of entertainment, as well as displays honoring Washington's history. The purpose of the fair was to celebrate the area's success and to attract more settlers and businesses to the Pacific Northwest. Nearly 4 million people attended the exposition.

The battleship USS *Nebraska* was launched from Seattle in October 1904.

This poster advertised the Alaska-Yukon-Pacific Exposition, which was held in Seattle in 1909.

While cities grew, many small towns and villages remained isolated. Communities farmed, fished, and ran their businesses, such as barber shops and restaurants. Hotels provided temporary housing for loggers and other workers.

Many of Washington's citizens worked in coal mines and logging camps. They worked in dangerous conditions for very little pay. New laws were eventually passed to improve working conditions.

In 1854, Arthur Denny, one of the founders of Seattle, proposed a measure at the first session of the territorial legislature granting women the right to vote in the Washington Territory. It did not pass. Until the early twentieth century, women throughout most of the United States were not allowed to vote. In 1910, Washington became the fifth state to give women this right. Washington acted ten years before the Nineteenth Amendment to the U.S. Constitution gave women nationwide the right to vote. In 1926, Bertha Landes was elected mayor of Seattle. She was the first woman to be elected mayor of a major American city.

Wars and Hard Times

During World War I (1914–1918), which the United States entered in 1917, more than 68,000 state residents served in the military. The United States government built Fort Lewis, one of the nation's largest army bases, in Pierce County.

When the Great Depression, a period of severe economic hardship, started in 1929, Washington's economy suffered. Four out of five lumber and paper mills closed. Tens of thousands of people lost their jobs. The federal government began a building program to improve lives and put people back to work. Huge dams were constructed on the Columbia River. These dams harnessed water power to produce electricity, prevented flooding, and created reservoirs to irrigate farmlands. The biggest was the Grand Coulee Dam, completed in 1941.

The Grand Coulee Dam has been called the "biggest thing built by the hands of man." Behind the dam is Lake Roosevelt, which is 151 miles (243 kilometers) long and stretches to the Canadian border. It took eight years to build the dam, which is the largest concrete structure in North America. It creates more electricity from water power than any other source in the nation.

World War II broke out in Europe in 1939. The United States entered the war after Japan attacked the U.S. naval base at Pearl Harbor in Hawaii on December 7, 1941. Washington's shipyards and aircraft manufacturers worked overtime to provide battleships and combat planes for the war. The electricity generated from the Grand Coulee Dam was especially helpful to the Washington industries that flourished during the war. In 1944, the Hanford Engineering Works in Richland became the top-secret site of plutonium production. It produced plutonium for some of the first atomic bombs. In August 1945, B-29 bombers produced by the Boeing Company in Seattle dropped atomic bombs on two Japanese cities. Japan surrendered by the next month, and the war ended.

GRAND COULEE DAM

The Grand Coulee Dam is nearly 1 mile (1.6 km) long. There is enough concrete in the dam to build a highway 60 feet (18 m) wide and 4 inches (10 cm) thick from Los Angeles to New York City.

Workers built the framework for tunnels inside the Grand Coulee Dam in 1937. The dam was completed in 1941.

World War II had especially devastating effects on the Japanese-American population living on the West Coast. After the attack on Pearl Harbor, many Japanese Americans living in the United States were suspected of spying for—or at the least being loyal to—Japan. In most cases, there was little or no proof showing that Japanese Americans were spies or were disloyal. In 1942, President Franklin D. Roosevelt signed an executive order that led to the imprisonment of more than 100,000 men, women, and children of Japanese descent. Japanese Americans living in Washington, California, and Oregon were affected by this order. They were forced to sell most of their possessions. They had to abandon their businesses and leave their homes.

The Japanese Americans were moved to internment camps set up in isolated regions away from the coast. The camps were surrounded by barbed-wire fences and patrolled by armed guards. Approximately 13,000 Japanese Americans from

Japanese-American families were moved to internment camps during World War II.

Washington were sent to the camps. No internee was charged with or convicted of any act of espionage. People were placed in the camps without due process of law as required by the U.S. Constitution. They were forced to remain at these internment camps until shortly before the war ended in 1945.

Postwar Prosperity

After the war, Boeing began to build jets made specifically for transporting passengers. Washington's economy flourished. The government built a series of dams on the Columbia and Snake rivers that produced electrical power and helped with flood control and the irrigation of dry land.

World's fairs brought more people to Washington. In 1962, Seattle hosted Century 21, a world's fair. More than 9 million people came to ride a futuristic monorail, to visit the Pacific Science Center, or to take in the view from the top of the Space Needle, a soaring 605-foot (184-m) structure built especially for the fair. In 1974, Spokane had its own world's fair, called Expo '74. The fair's

Seattle's Space Needle was built for a world's fair in 1962.

theme was a safe and clean environment. During the 1970s and 1980s, environmental cleanup became an important issue in the state. Washington was one of the first states in the country to start a recycling program.

Washington Today

Washington's population grew by almost 735,000 between 1980 and 1990, as new electronics and computer companies brought many jobs to the state. But by the beginning of the twenty-first century, Washington's economic boom had slowed down.

In early 2002, Washington and Oregon had the highest unemployment rates in the United States. Agricultural jobs in eastern Washington disappeared. As more people moved to the area, competition for jobs became harder.

In 2008 and 2009, Washington's economy took more of a tumble. The United States was in a severe economic recession, and many of the state's largest employers laid off workers. In some ways, though, Washington was better off than other states. A large share of the state's income comes from trade. About one-quarter of the residents are involved in trading diverse goods with other states and countries. Many of these jobs remained stable even in tough economic times.

Important Dates

★ **1592** Greek explorer Juan de Fuca sails along the coast of what is now Washington.

★ **1792** American Robert Gray travels up the Columbia River.

★ **1805** Explorers Lewis and Clark reach the Pacific Ocean.

★ **1811** John Jacob Astor establishes Fort Okanogan.

★ **1846** The British move out of the part of the Oregon Country south of the 49th parallel.

★ **1847** Cayuse Indians attack the Whitman mission, killing fourteen people.

★ **1848** The Oregon Territory, which includes Washington, Idaho, and parts of Montana and Wyoming, is established.

★ **1853** The Washington Territory splits from the Oregon Territory.

★ **1855–1858** Indian wars are fought.

★ **1883** The Northern Pacific railroad line between St. Louis and Tacoma is completed.

★ **1889** Washington becomes the forty-second state on November 11.

★ **1897** The Klondike Gold Rush turns Seattle into a boomtown.

★ **1926** Bertha Landes is elected mayor of Seattle.

★ **1941** The Grand Coulee Dam is completed.

★ **1944** The Hanford Engineering Works becomes a center of plutonium production for nuclear weapons.

★ **1962** The Space Needle is built in Seattle.

★ **1980** Mount Saint Helens, a volcanic mountain, erupts.

★ **2001** An earthquake registering 6.8 on the Richter scale shakes Seattle and Puget Sound.

★ **2004** Mount Saint Helens erupts again; the eruption continues for four years.

★ **2009** During a record heat wave, the temperature in Seattle reaches 103 °F (39 °C) for the first time in recorded history.

The People

According to U.S. Census Bureau estimates, about 80 percent of Washington's population is white. Some of these residents are descendants of American and European settlers who came to the state many years ago. Others may be more recent immigrants from European countries such as Germany, Great Britain, Ireland, or the Scandinavian countries. People of Hispanic descent make up more than 9 percent of the population. Many of these residents are from Mexico. Asian Americans make up about 7 percent of the population. More than 3 percent of Washingtonians are African American, and 1.4 percent of the population is American Indian. Regardless of percentages, the different cultures that can be found in Washington have helped to make the state what it is today.

The First Residents

American Indians were the first people to live in the region now known as Washington. Today, there are about 89,000 American Indians living in Washington. Many of them live on more than twenty reservations across the state. Part of the Confederated Tribes of the Umatilla Indian reservation is found in the southeastern section of the state. This reservation is home to the Cayuse, Walla Walla, and Umatilla tribes. The Colville Indian reservation is in north-central Washington.

Children pose in front of the Space Needle in Seattle.

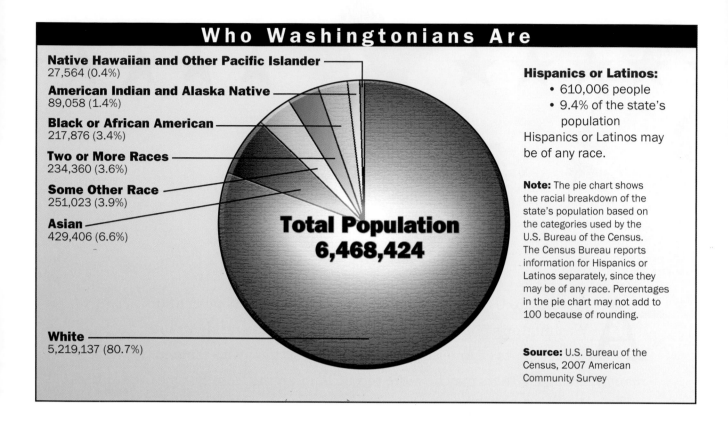

Who Washingtonians Are

Native Hawaiian and Other Pacific Islander
27,564 (0.4%)

American Indian and Alaska Native
89,058 (1.4%)

Black or African American
217,876 (3.4%)

Two or More Races
234,360 (3.6%)

Some Other Race
251,023 (3.9%)

Asian
429,406 (6.6%)

White
5,219,137 (80.7%)

Total Population 6,468,424

Hispanics or Latinos:
- 610,006 people
- 9.4% of the state's population

Hispanics or Latinos may be of any race.

Note: The pie chart shows the racial breakdown of the state's population based on the categories used by the U.S. Bureau of the Census. The Census Bureau reports information for Hispanics or Latinos separately, since they may be of any race. Percentages in the pie chart may not add to 100 because of rounding.

Source: U.S. Bureau of the Census, 2007 American Community Survey

South-central Washington is home to the reservation of the Yakama people. The reservation spreads across more than one million acres (405,000 hectares) of protected land along the Cascade Mountains. It is one of the largest Indian reservations in the United States. The reservation is home to the Yakama Nation Museum and Cultural Center. The center houses a museum, restaurant, theater, research center, and library.

Many of Washington's American Indian nations are

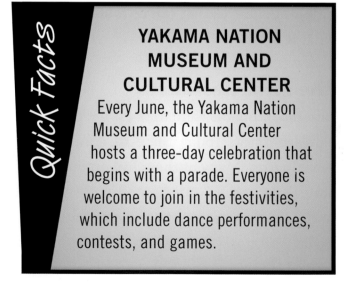

Quick Facts

YAKAMA NATION MUSEUM AND CULTURAL CENTER
Every June, the Yakama Nation Museum and Cultural Center hosts a three-day celebration that begins with a parade. Everyone is welcome to join in the festivities, which include dance performances, contests, and games.

This photo shows a member of the Umatilla tribe in 1910. Today, American Indians make up 1.4 percent of Washington's population.

interested in sharing their history and culture with others. Throughout the year, meetings and festivals are held across the state. Many Washington tribes, as well as tribes from other parts of the country, join in the festivities.

These children on the Yakama reservation are picking huckleberries.

Ballard: A Slice of Scandinavia

Scandinavian immigrants settled the fishing and lumbering town of Ballard in the 1880s. In 1907, Ballard became part of Seattle, and today it is one of the city's most colorful and historic neighborhoods. Ballard's Nordic roots can be seen in its many businesses specializing in selling Scandinavian foods and gift items. The Nordic Heritage Museum opened in 1980 and claims to be the only museum in the United States that celebrates the story of immigrants from all five Nordic countries (Denmark, Norway, Sweden, Finland, and Iceland). Leif Erikson Lodge hosts events that promote, preserve, and celebrate the heritage of Norway.

The Nordic Heritage Museum in Ballard hosts festivals that celebrate Norway's heritage.

Asian Americans

Asian Americans have had a troubled history in Washington. In the 1870s and 1880s, many Chinese immigrants suffered when anti-Chinese riots destroyed their homes and businesses. Some Chinese immigrants were even killed. These anti-Chinese sentiments were a result of tough competition for employment. Many American workers felt that these new immigrants were stealing their jobs. In 1885, a mob of Tacoma's leading citizens, including the mayor, forced Chinese residents to leave their homes. Most of these residents were so afraid for their lives that they never returned. Many relocated to Portland, Oregon. In 1993, the Tacoma City Council passed a resolution to express regret for this poor treatment. The Chinese Reconciliation Project Foundation was founded in 1994. Some of the foundation's purposes are to educate the community about multicultural history and to encourage all residents to celebrate their diversity and their common qualities. In 2005, the foundation helped build Chinese Reconciliation Park, a commemorative park for all Tacoma residents.

Before and during World War II, Washington's Japanese-American residents also faced difficult times in the state. Takuji Yamashita was born in Japan but later moved to the United States and attended the University of Washington School of Law. In 1902, he graduated and passed the bar exam with honors. But he was not allowed to practice law. At that time all attorneys had to be U.S. citizens, and federal law barred virtually all immigrants from Asia from becoming citizens. (It was not until 1952 that Congress changed the law to allow Japanese immigrants to become U.S. citizens.) Yamashita went to court to argue for his rights, but he did not win his case. Unable to make a living as an attorney, Yamashita opened a restaurant. He later returned to Japan and died there in 1959.

In 2001, the state supreme court declared Takuji Yamashita an honorary lawyer. It was a symbolic and important gesture. "This is the spirit of my great-grandfather," said one relative who is a high school teacher. "He taught me to never give up."

In Seattle, a Chinese American named Wing Luke became the first Asian American to hold an elected office in the state when he won a council seat in 1962. It was another sign that the state was moving away from its troubled history.

Today, the Asian-American population in Washington is growing. Besides people of Chinese and Japanese heritage, there are many Vietnamese, Filipino, Laotian, Korean, Indian, and Thai Americans. In 1996, Gary Locke was elected governor of Washington. He was the first Chinese American to become a state governor in the United States. In 2009, Locke became the first Chinese American to hold the office of U.S. Secretary of Commerce.

MAKING A FOLDING FAN

Folding fans are an important part of Japan's history and culture. Many Japanese people who moved to Washington brought these prized belongings to the state. Today, Japanese and Japanese Americans in Washington still treasure these traditional fans. By following these instructions, you can design and make your very own fan.

WHAT YOU NEED

One piece of ordinary typing or printer paper

Markers

Ruler

Six 12-inch (30-cm) pipe cleaners

Adhesive tape

About 12 inches (30 cm) of narrow ribbon

Fold the paper in half so it is 4½ inches (11.4 cm) wide and 11 inches (28 cm) long. Decorate one side with markers, with the folded edge as the top. Many fans had pictures of gardens, with hanging trees, ponds, and small bridges, but feel free to create your own design.

Open the paper to the blank inside. Lay the ruler along the 11-inch (28-cm) edge. Measure and mark every inch (2.5 cm) along this edge (ten marks). Do the same to the opposite edge. Using a dark marker, draw a line from the top mark to the opposite one on the bottom edge, making ten sections. You can use the edge of the ruler to keep your lines straight.

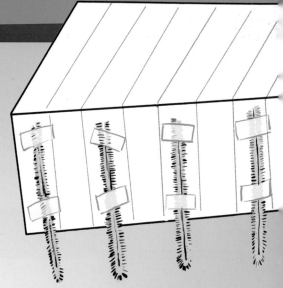

Fold the pipe cleaners neatly in half. Starting with the first section, lay a folded pipe cleaner in every other section, between the lines. The pointy ends should face the top of the paper. Position the pipe cleaners so the points are all just a little bit lower than the fold in the paper. Tape the pipe cleaners down to the paper. Make sure to keep their ends closed. Close the paper by folding it in half again, over the pipe cleaners. The drawing you made should be facing you. Tape the left and right edges closed.

Now turn the paper over and look through the side without decorations. Find the line marking the first section. Make a fold there. At the next line, fold the paper the opposite way, so you are pleating the paper back and forth. Keep it up until you have made ten folds.

Thread the ribbon through the pipe cleaners at the bottom and pull closed. Tie it with a double knot. You can trim or curl the ends of the ribbon, or tie a bow.

Try opening and closing your fan. You can use it next time the room gets too hot!

Education in Washington

When Washington was made a territory in 1853, American settlers had established only five schools in the region. Today, there are about two thousand public schools in the state and more than sixty places of higher learning. Whitman Seminary, named after the famous missionaries, was the first school of higher education to open—in 1859 in Walla Walla. It was renamed Whitman College in 1882. The University of Washington opened in 1861 in Seattle, and is one of the oldest universities on the West Coast. It is the largest university

There are about 2,000 public schools in Washington.

Governor Chris Gregoire, shown here reading to a group of children, has worked hard to improve Washington's schools.

in the state. The school's sports teams are nicknamed the Huskies. The football team is often led onto the field by an Alaskan Malamute.

More adults in Washington have graduated from high school than in many other states. Still, the state government has worked to improve the education system in recent years. The Washington Reading Corps is for students who need help with reading. Governor Chris Gregoire earned her teaching certificate from the University of Washington. She has made education a priority, expanding all-day kindergarten and creating programs to ensure better math and science teaching and learning.

Famous Washingtonians

Chief Seattle: American Indian Leader

Born in the 1780s, Chief Seattle was the leader of the Duwamish and Suquamish American Indian tribes living in the Puget Sound region. When the first white settlers arrived, he made friends with them and signed an important treaty, which established two reservations for American Indians. When other tribes went to war against the settlers in 1855, Chief Seattle remained at peace with them. But he did express his doubts about what the settlers would do with the land they hoped to buy from him. Seattle's memory lives on in the great city, Seattle, which was named in his honor.

Bing Crosby: Entertainer

Born Harry Lillis Crosby in Tacoma in 1903, Bing Crosby was a famous singer and movie star. Crosby acted in more than fifty movies and recorded more than one thousand songs. One of his most popular songs was "White Christmas," which was written for the movie *Holiday Inn*. Crosby won an Academy Award in 1944 for his role in the movie *Going My Way*. Bing Crosby died in 1977.

Dixy Lee Ray: Scientist, Educator, and Governor

Washington's first woman governor, Dixy Lee Ray was born in Tacoma in 1914. Ray became a marine biologist and taught at the University of Washington for twenty-seven years. In 1973, President Richard Nixon appointed her to head the U.S. Atomic Energy Commission (AEC). Ray was enthusiastic but also cautious about nuclear power. She was elected governor of Washington in 1976 and served until 1981.

Gary Locke: Politician

The first Chinese-American governor in the United States, Gary Locke was born in Seattle in 1950. Locke worked in his father's grocery store as a youth and received a degree in political science from Yale University in 1972. He was elected to the state house of representatives in 1982, where he supported improvements in public education and better environmental protection. Elected governor in 1996, Locke served two four-year terms. President Barack Obama appointed him U.S. Secretary of Commerce in 2009.

Bill Gates: Business Leader and Computer Whiz

Bill Gates was born in Seattle in 1955 and met his future business partner Paul Allen in the eighth grade. At age seventeen, Gates and Allen started their own company. A few years later, Gates entered Harvard University, where he and Allen developed a computer language for personal computers. Soon after they founded the Microsoft Corporation, Gates dropped out of Harvard to run his growing company. In 1987, at age thirty-one, Bill Gates became the youngest American self-made billionaire.

Hilary Swank: Actor

Hilary Swank was born in 1974 and grew up in Bellingham. She competed in the Junior Olympics, ranked fifth in the state in gymnastics, and swam in the Washington State Championships. Her breakout roles in *The Next Karate Kid* and *Beverly Hills, 90210* launched her career. She has been awarded more than thirty acting awards, including two Academy Awards and two Golden Globes. She is perhaps best known for her performance as a boxer in *Million Dollar Baby*.

A Great Place to Live

From 1990 to 2000, the state's population increased by about one million. In 1990, it was the eighteenth state in population. In 2000, it ranked fifteenth. By 2007, the state had gained more than another half-million people, reaching a population of almost 6.5 million and ranking thirteenth. About three out of every four Washingtonians live west of the Cascade Mountains. More than half of the state's population lives in the Puget Sound region. Why do so many people want to live in Washington? They like its natural beauty, its mild climate, the friendly residents, and the different types of job opportunities.

Sports and Recreation

The people of Washington love to play and watch sports. Seattle is home to the Seahawks football team and the Seattle Storm women's basketball team. Seattle's baseball team, the Mariners, got a new ballpark in 1999. Safeco Field has a retractable roof and cost more than half a billion dollars.

Hydroplane racing is a popular sport in Puget Sound. Every summer during Seattle's Seafair, thousands of locals and tourists come to watch the Unlimited Hydroplane Races on Lake

Seattle has a women's basketball team, the Seattle Storm, shown here in a game against the Los Angeles Sparks.

A mother and her two children look up at a giant red cedar tree in Olympic National Park.

Washington. These lightweight boats shoot across the water at speeds up to 200 miles (320 km) per hour. Part of the fun of watching is getting sprayed by the water these "flying boats" leave in their wake.

Washington has three national parks. The largest is Mount Rainier National Park. Olympic National Park, in the far northwestern part of the state, is one of the most varied national parks in the country. Within its borders, it has rain forests, lakes, glaciers, and 57 miles (92 km) of untouched coastline. The state also boasts nine national forests, and more than one hundred state parks and historical sites. People go to these places to hike, camp, fish, hunt, bike, and just to relax.

Places to Visit

Washington is proud of its city parks as well as its national and state parks. Tacoma's Point Defiance Park is one of the largest city parks in the United States. Visitors can enjoy hiking trails, a zoo, a replica of a logging camp from the early 1900s, and Fort Nisqually, the first fur-trading outpost on Puget Sound of the Hudson's Bay Company. Manito Park in Spokane has a number of colorful flowering gardens, including a Japanese garden. Riverfront Park is just as impressive. It features waterfalls from the Spokane River and some of the attractions from Expo '74, including the U.S. Pavilion.

Washington is known for its great outdoors, but there are great things to do indoors, too. For those visitors who enjoy classical music, the Seattle Symphony is an important part of Washington's cultural scene. The Seattle Repertory Theatre is famous for its staging of old and new plays.

Seattle is proud of its many fine museums. The Burke Museum of Natural History and Culture is located on the University of Washington campus. The Seattle Asian Art Museum has one of the best collections of Asian art in the country. The Museum of Flight has more than fifty aircraft on display. Among them are the first presidential jet and an Apollo space command module. The Seattle Aquarium has an Underwater Dome that holds 400,000 gallons (1.5 million liters) of water. The Experience Music Project/Science Fiction Museum and Hall of Fame is devoted to the history and exploration of popular music and science fiction. It is home to permanent and featured exhibitions, interactive installations, educational experiences, and special programs.

Tacoma is the home of the Washington State History Museum, which includes a special interactive section of hands-on exhibits. There are also many

Harrison Street / Group Entrance

This building is part of the Experience Music Project/Science Fiction Museum and Hall of Fame in Seattle.

other museums across the state. The World Kite Museum and Hall of Fame is in Long Beach. Visitors who want to learn more about Lewis and Clark can go to the Lewis and Clark Interpretive Center in Fort Canby State Park.

Calendar of Events

★ **The Great Bavarian Ice Fest in Leavenworth**

This winter festival is held in January and features dogsled rides, a snowshoe race, and an ice-cube hunt for children. Another highlight is the Northwest Regional Dog Sled Pulling Competition.

★ **The Upper Skagit Bald Eagle Festival**

In late January or early February, thousands of people travel to the Upper Skagit River Valley to see one of the largest winter gatherings of bald eagles in the country. Visitors can also attend lectures, storytelling, and music concerts.

★ **The Cherry Blossom and Japanese Cultural Festival in Seattle**

This annual event takes place in April and celebrates Japanese art and culture in the Pacific Northwest.

★ **Washington State Apple Blossom Festival in Wenatchee**

Held in April, this eleven-day festival has parades, a scholarship auction, and a children's art contest and exhibition.

★ **The Port Townsend Blues and Heritage Festival**

Every summer, leading blues musicians and singers gather in Port Townsend to perform and conduct musical workshops.

★ Yakima Treaty Days in Toppenish

This American Indian celebration is held every June to commemorate the anniversary of the signing of the 1855 treaty. Toppenish is located in the Yakama Indian Reservation in southeast Washington.

★ Seafair in Seattle

The biggest community festival in the Pacific Northwest, Seafair takes place from early July through early August. Popular events include a milk carton derby, a torchlight parade, and the famed Unlimited Hydroplane Races on Lake Washington.

★ The Western Washington State Fair in Puyallup

Sometimes called the Puyallup Fair, this is one of the ten largest fairs in North America. It runs for seventeen days every September. Visitors can enjoy rides, concerts, livestock shows, and rodeos—and kids can even test their skills at riding sheep.

★ The Ellensburg Rodeo

Started in September 1923, the Ellensburg Rodeo is one of the most popular rodeos in the country.

Members of the Yakama Indian Nation start off each evening's events with a traditional dance in the arena.

★ The Jules Fest in Poulsbo

In December, this Norwegian holiday tradition features a local girl dressed as the Lucia Bride, who lights the Christmas tree. She is followed by Santa Claus, who listens as the children tell him what they want for Christmas.

How the Government Works

The basic structure of Washington's government, as well as rules about how government operates and what it can or cannot do, are established by the state constitution, which was created in 1889 at the time Washington became a state. This constitution has been amended, or revised, over the years, but it remains the foundation of government in the state.

The center of Washington's state government is Olympia, the state capital. In addition to its state government, Washington has many local governments. The state is divided into thirty-nine counties. Most of these counties are governed by a board of county commissioners. The three commissioners in each county are assisted by a number of other officials. They include a county clerk, a treasurer, and a sheriff. There are 281 cities and towns in Washington. Most of them are governed by a mayor and a city council. The elected mayors and council members serve four-year terms. Some cities in Washington are run by a city manager instead of a mayor.

The Capital

Olympia was named Washington's capital when Washington became a territory in 1853. It is located at the southern end of Puget Sound. It was known by different names to the American Indians who lived there for many generations and to the first European settlers. It was renamed for the Olympic Mountains

Elected officials meet at Washington's State Capitol in Olympia.

Branches of Government

EXECUTIVE ★ ★ ★ ★ ★ ★ ★ ★ ★ ★ ★ ★ ★ ★ ★ ★ ★ ★ ★

The executive branch includes the governor, lieutenant governor, secretary of state, treasurer, and attorney general. The governor is head of the executive branch. He or she either approves or rejects laws passed by the legislature. The governor also makes up the state budget each year and appoints officials to government departments and agencies. Elected officials in the executive branch serve four-year terms. They do not have a limit on the number of terms they can serve.

LEGISLATIVE ★ ★ ★ ★ ★ ★ ★ ★ ★ ★ ★ ★ ★ ★ ★ ★ ★ ★

Washington's legislature, or lawmaking body, is called the general assembly. It is made up of two houses. The house of representatives has ninety-eight members. The state senate has forty-nine members. Members of the house of representatives serve two-year terms and may not serve more than six of the previous twelve years. Members of the senate serve four-year terms and cannot hold office for more than eight of the previous fourteen years. No legislator can serve in the general assembly for more than fourteen of the previous twenty years. Legislators propose and pass laws for the state. Any proposed law must be passed by a majority vote in both houses of the legislature before it goes to the governor for executive approval.

JUDICIAL ★

The judicial branch interprets and enforces the laws of the state. Washington's court system ranges from municipal (city), district (county), and superior (state) courts up to the state supreme court. When a defendant or plaintiff first protests, or appeals, the outcome of a case in municipal, district, or superior court, the case goes to a court of appeals, which can uphold or overturn a lower court's rulings. Court of appeals decisions may be further appealed to the highest state court—the supreme court. The supreme court is made up of nine judges who are elected to serve six-year terms. Judges for the court of appeals are also elected to serve six-year terms. District court judges are elected to four-year terms. Municipal court and superior court judges can be elected or appointed to serve four-year terms.

Quick Facts

WASHINGTON'S REPRESENTATIVES IN CONGRESS

In 2010, Washington had nine representatives in the U.S. House of Representatives. Like all states, it has two senators in the U.S. Senate.

northwest of the city. Olympia has about 45,000 people and is considered a small capital city. The governor's residence is located in Olympia. The building where lawmakers meet, the Temple of Justice building where the supreme court hears cases, and the beautiful grounds with Japanese cherry trees are often called the Capitol Campus.

How a Bill Becomes a Law

Did you ever wonder how state laws are made? Citizens in Washington can play a key part in this decision making. If a citizen has an idea for a law, he or she can suggest it to representatives in the general assembly. Sometimes voters will collect many signatures from other voters who share their opinions on an idea. Then they present this petition about a proposed law to legislators. Members of the general assembly also come up with ideas for new laws.

A proposed law is called a bill. Wherever the idea originates, a representative or

Visitors to the State Capitol in Olympia can take a tour of the building.

person on the representative's staff takes the idea and actually writes a bill. A bill can be introduced first in the house of representatives or in the senate. If the bill starts in the house of representatives, the president of the house of representatives assigns a committee to review the bill. The members of the committee hold hearings and discuss the bill. If they agree that it should be a law, they send it back to the house of representatives. The entire house of representatives then votes on the bill. If the bill is approved by a majority vote, it is sent to the state senate. The senate follows a procedure similar to the one in the house of representatives. A committee considers the bill, and if it is approved by the committee, then the entire senate votes on whether to approve it.

When both parts of the legislature have approved a bill, it is sent to the governor. If the governor approves, the bill becomes a law. However, if the governor rejects—or vetoes—the bill, the house and senate still have a chance to pass it. If the house and senate both vote in favor of the bill again—this time by a two-thirds majority—the governor's veto can be overturned, and the bill becomes a law.

Laws from the People

Throughout history, Washingtonians have shown that they can make a difference. On Mother's Day in 1909, Sonora Louise Smart Dodd's interest was sparked by a sermon given at her church in Spokane. Dodd loved her father and wondered why there was no official day to honor fathers. She took her idea to local ministers, and they supported it. She then brought the idea before the local government in Spokane. The government leaders liked it, too. Dodd chose a Sunday in June for Father's Day because that was the month in which her father

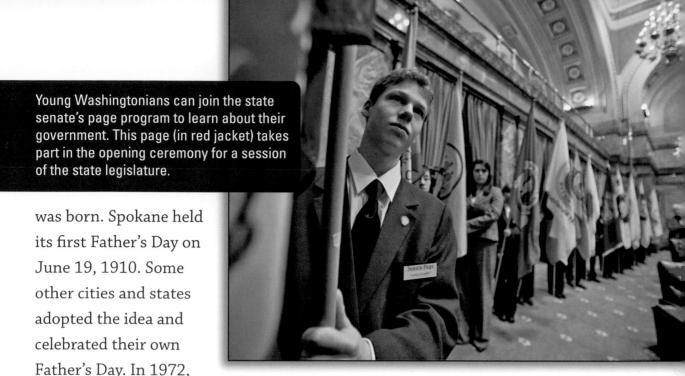

Young Washingtonians can join the state senate's page program to learn about their government. This page (in red jacket) takes part in the opening ceremony for a session of the state legislature.

was born. Spokane held its first Father's Day on June 19, 1910. Some other cities and states adopted the idea and celebrated their own Father's Day. In 1972, President Richard Nixon declared that the third Sunday in June was permanently set as a day to honor fathers nationwide.

Sometimes kids can help make new laws, too. In 1997, a group of students from Crestwood Elementary School in Kent, Washington, suggested to state legislators that Washington should have a state insect. The legislature agreed to allow school students to decide what the state insect should be. About 25,000 students from more than one hundred school districts voted. They chose the green darner dragonfly, which is also called the mosquito hawk. The students voted for this insect because it can be found all over Washington and helps the environment by eating insect pests such as mosquitoes. In 1997, the common green darner dragonfly was officially proclaimed the state insect of Washington.

That is just one example of how young Washingtonians can take part in their government. By staying informed about local issues and current events, you can decide how you would like to help. Volunteering for a campaign or spending some time helping groups who are trying to have a bill passed are just two of the many ways you can help your community. As Governor Chris Gregoire has said, "This is a tremendous opportunity for more Washingtonians to become more involved in their communities. . . . People really can make a difference. When we give our time and our effort, we build stronger communities."

Making a Living

Washington has a varied economy. Plentiful rainfall or good irrigation systems, as well as rich soil, make much of the state perfect for farming. The western region's mild climate has attracted many businesses to this corner of America. A number of large companies have made their headquarters in Washington. Boeing, one of the world's largest producers of airplanes, has locations in Bellevue, Everett, Issaquah, Kent, Renton, Seattle, Spokane, and other cities.. The headquarters for the Costco warehouse store chain is in Issaquah. Redmond is the base for the computer software giant Microsoft. Seattle is home to the Nordstrom department-store chain, the Starbucks Coffee Company, and the online retailer Amazon.com.

Riches from the Earth

Washington is first when it comes to many farm products. The state produces more pears, sweet cherries, red raspberries, lentils, and hops than any other state. The hop plant is used in making beer, medicines, and other products. Washington is second among the states in the production of potatoes, peas, apricots, and asparagus. Most of the fruits and vegetables are grown in central Washington. This region was once too dry for growing crops, but irrigation turned it into fertile farmland. The dry air cuts down on insect pests that threaten fruit trees.

Farming is an important part of Washington's economy.

Washington produces more apples than any other state.

The first apples arrived in Washington on a sailing ship in 1825. Soon pioneers were growing apple trees from the seeds. The first commercial apple orchards appeared around 1889. Today, there are more than 153,000 acres (62,000 ha) of apple orchards in central Washington. The state's orchards produce about 6 billion pounds (2.7 billion kg) of apples each year, more than any other state. Most of these apples are grown in the eastern foothills of the Cascade Mountains. The soil there is rich in lava-ash, which is good for growing crops, and there is plenty of sunshine and cool mountain water.

RECIPE FOR CARAMEL APPLES

Washington is known for its apples. Apples are a delicious plain, of course. But why not dress them up with a little caramel? This Halloween treat can be enjoyed throughout the year.

WHAT YOU NEED

Red Delicious apples

Popsicle sticks, or anything that will work as a handle

1 bag caramels

2 tablespoons (30 milliliters) water

Wash and dry the apples. It is hard to say how many you will need. You can start with four, but you may use more. It depends on how much caramel sauce you make. Push a Popsicle stick into the top of each apple to create a handle. Set these aside on a large piece of wax paper while you make the caramel sauce.

Mix the caramel and the water in a dish that is safe to use in a microwave. Microwave the mixture for 3 to 4 minutes. If you want to use a regular stove, melt the caramel and water in a 1½-quart (1.4-liter) saucepan for about 20 minutes over low to medium heat. Ask an adult for help with the stove. When the caramel starts to melt, stir the mixture gently until it is smooth.

When the mixture is ready, dip the apples into the caramel sauce. Place them on the wax paper, and chill them in the refrigerator. When the caramel has hardened, eat and enjoy.

There is a good chance that the flower bulbs many Americans plant each fall came from Washington. Tulip, iris, and other flower bulbs are cultivated there and then shipped across the country.

Dairy farms flourish in western Washington. There are also many cattle and sheep ranches in the eastern part of the state, where the flat grasslands are perfect for grazing.

Mining is another important part of the state's economy. Washington's most important mineral is coal. Most of the coal mines are located in the southwestern part of the state. Other minerals mined in Washington include magnesium, zinc, limestone, sand and gravel, and silver.

Tulip bulbs are cultivated in Washington, then shipped to other parts of the country.

The flat grasslands of eastern Washington are good for raising sheep.

Logging was one of the first industries in Washington. The state's great forests are still being harvested. Some of the logs are taken to mills where they are cut into lumber for building. Other mills turn wood into paper products. The only states that produce more lumber are California and Oregon.

Wealth from the Sea

Washingtonians love their salmon—baked, broiled, or marinated. No state except Alaska catches and packages more of this delicious, pink-fleshed fish. There are more than two hundred other edible fish and shellfish caught in Pacific coastal waters and inland rivers. Commercial fishing provides the state with millions of dollars each year.

The oyster beds near Olympia are among the finest in North America. The Olympia oyster is a Washington delicacy. These small oysters are about 2 inches (5 cm) across. Razor clams are another favorite. Thousands of clam diggers come to beaches to dig up these clams. But there is a fifteen-razor-clam limit. Digging for razor clams can be a challenge because, unlike most other clams, the razor clam can "run away." It elongates its body out of its shell and burrows deep down in the sand.

Pike Place Fish Market, in downtown Seattle, displays fresh fish for sale. Commercial fishing earns millions of dollars for Washington every year.

Tourist Dollars

Washington's natural beauty and its many other attractions make it a top state for tourism. In 2008, the tourism industry earned about $15.7 billion. There is even an Academy of Hospitality and Tourism program in some high schools in Seattle. Students learn about the tourism industry and job opportunities in that field. They study travel subjects and go on field trips.

Making Things

Almost 342,000 workers in the state are employed in manufacturing. The biggest industry is the manufacturing of transportation equipment, especially aircraft and equipment for aerospace travel. Nearly one-third of these workers are employed by the Boeing Company. The Boeing plant in Everett covers 60 acres (24 ha) and is ten stories high. It is one of the largest enclosed spaces in the world. It has to be large enough to fit the wide-body jumbo passenger jets that are assembled there.

The Boeing Company provides jobs for many Washingtonians.

The shipbuilding industry is centered in Seattle, Bremerton, and Tacoma. Other important goods made in Washington include paper, industrial machinery, precision instruments, and printed materials from brochures to newspapers.

Computer software, data-storage, and other high-tech companies have become big business in Washington in the past thirty years. In addition to Microsoft's headquarters in Redmond, the state hosts several other companies in the computer and technology industries. Bothell hosts Lockheed Martin Aculight, which creates lasers. Seattle is home to two research and development offices for Google and an office for Adobe software developers.

Products & Resources

Cherries

Washington produces more sweet cherries than any other state. Besides red cherries, Washington farmers also grow black and yellow cherries.

Lumber

Trees cut down in Washington's forests are converted into lumber for building. The pulp is also used for various paper products, including newspaper.

Starbucks

Starbucks Coffee opened its first store in 1971 in Seattle's Pike Place Market. The company expanded rapidly. In 2010, there were more than 16,000 Starbucks coffee shops in about fifty countries worldwide. In addiction to coffee, most Starbucks shops sell food, gifts, and music. Starbucks products, including bottled coffee drinks and ice cream, are carried in many grocery stores.

Amazon.com

The Seattle-based company Amazon.com revolutionized the way books are sold. Amazon was one of the first Internet retailers and is now one of the most popular shopping sites. It was among the first companies to develop an electronic book reader, the Kindle.

Tourism

Each year, the state makes billions of dollars from tourism. Visitors come to take in the sights and experience all that the state has to offer. The tourism industry also keeps many Washingtonians employed.

Trading Goods

Washington's export trade is very important to the state economy. Exports are goods that are sent from one source to other places. According to the Washington State Office of Community, Trade and Economic Development, Washington exported more than $66 billion worth of goods in 2008. The state is the fourth largest exporter in the country. Washington exports items such as computer software, transportation and aerospace materials, electronic and scientific equipment, wood products, and crops. Washington's location plays a major part in its international exporting success. The state exports products to many countries including China, Canada, Japan, the United Arab Emirates, Ireland, Mexico, and the United Kingdom. When goods are being exported to Europe using planes, Washington companies can use North Pole air routes that make the travel time shorter. The state has a lot of coastline with many ports. By ship, Washington is closer to Asian ports than any other port on the West Coast.

Washington is the fourth largest exporter in the country. Many different kinds of goods are shipped from the Port of Seattle, shown here.

Workers & Industries

Industry	Number of People Working in That Industry	Percentage of All Workers Who Are Working in That Industry
Education and health care	628,558	20%
Wholesale and retail businesses	465,528	15%
Publishing, media, entertainment, hotels, and restaurants	363,815	12%
Professionals, scientists, and managers	357,317	11%
Manufacturing	341,958	11%
Construction	254,644	8%
Banking and finance, insurance, and real estate	199,086	6%
Government	159,350	5%
Transportation and public utilities	156,716	5%
Other services	135,032	4%
Farming, fishing, forestry, and mining	76,228	2%
Totals	**3,138,232**	**100%**

Notes: Figures above do not include people in the armed forces. "Professionals" includes people such as doctors and lawyers. Percentages may not add to 100 because of rounding.

Source: U.S. Bureau of the Census, 2007 estimates

By ship, Washington is closer to Asian ports than any other port on the West Coast. The inlet of Puget Sound provides protected harbors for ships.

Washington also sends goods to its neighboring states and other states across the country. The same trade routes allow the state to import, or bring in, goods from other places.

Saving Energy

Running the complex machines of Washington's many industries requires a great deal of energy. Washington's power companies are at the forefront of finding new ways to save energy and to produce electricity using new technologies that do not cause pollution. Seattle City Light, the power company for Seattle, has become well known for its efforts in energy conservation. How do this company and other energy companies conserve so much energy? One way is by, in effect, paying consumers to use less electricity. Avista Utilities in Spokane is giving its customers rebates when they buy energy-efficient equipment. Another way is by letting people pay less for electricity when they use it during low-demand times, such as at night. Washington's energy companies produce electricity using wind and water power, which do not cause air pollution, and they encourage customers to install solar panels. In most cases, the companies will pay customers for "extra" electricity—generated by solar panels—that customers do not need for themselves and send to their power company.

Innovative ideas and the hard work of dedicated Washingtonians continue to prepare the state for the future, in the twenty-first century and beyond.

State Flag & Seal

The state flag is green with the official state seal in the center.

Washington's state seal is a portrait of George Washington. The words "The Seal of the State of Washington" are printed around the portrait. The year that Washington became a state, 1889, is at the bottom.

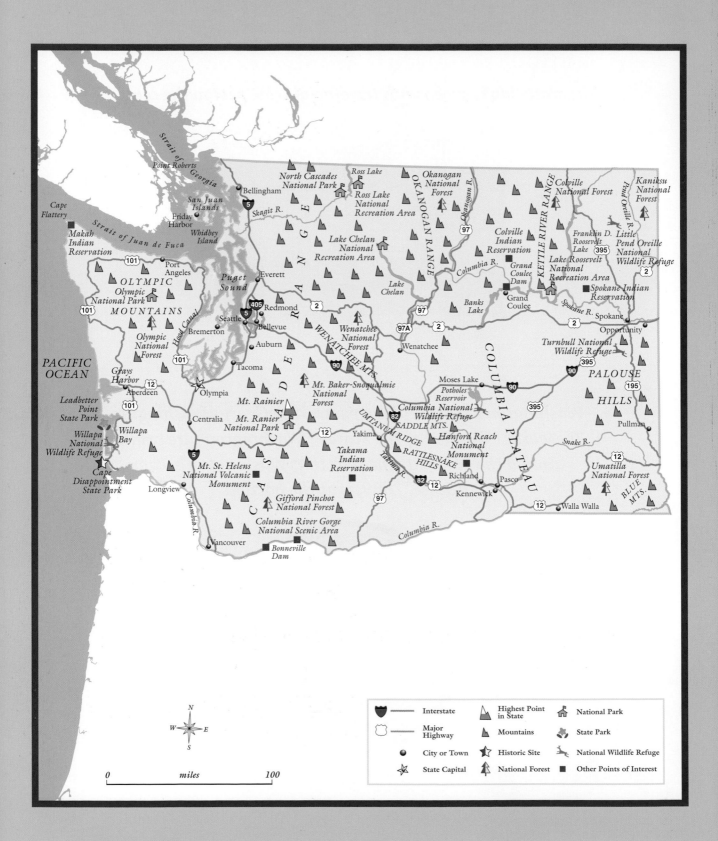

Point Roberts

Strait of Georgia

Cape
Flattery

Strait of Juan de Fuca

San Juan
Islands

Friday
Harbor

Whidbey
Island

Bellingham

Skagit R.

North Cascades
National Park

Ross Lake

Ross Lake
National
Recreation Area

Okanogan
National
Forest

Kaniksu
National
Forest

Colville
National Forest

KETTLE RIVER RANGE

Pend Oreille R.

Makah
Indian
Reservation

Port
Angeles

101

OLYMPIC

Olympic
National Park

MOUNTAINS

Puget
Sound

Everett

Lake Chelan
National
Recreation Area

OKANOGAN RANGE

Columbia R.

97

Colville
Indian
Reservation

Lake
Chelan

Banks
Lake

Grand
Coulee
Dam

Franklin D.
Roosevelt
Lake

Lake Roosevelt
National
Recreation Area

395

Little
Pend Oreille
National
Wildlife Refuge

2

101

Hood Canal

Seattle

405

5

Redmond

Bellevue

Auburn

Olympic
National Forest

Bremerton

RANGE

2

97A

97

Grand
Coulee

Spokane R.

Spokane Indian
Reservation

Spokane

2

Opportunity

PACIFIC
OCEAN

Grays
Harbor

Tacoma

Aberdeen

12

Olympia

Centralia

Mt. Rainier

Mt. Ranier
National Park

CASCADE

WENATCHEE MTS.

90

Wenatchee
National
Forest

97A

Wenatchee

Mt. Baker-Snoqualmie
National
Forest

COLUMBIA
PLATEAU

Turnbull National
Wildlife Refuge

90

395

PALOUSE

HILLS

195

Leadbetter
Point
State Park

Willapa
National
Wildlife Refuge

Willapa
Bay

5

Cape
Disappointment
State Park

Longview

Columbia R.

Vancouver

Mt. St. Helens
National Volcanic
Monument

Gifford Pinchot
National Forest

Columbia River Gorge
National Scenic Area

Bonneville
Dam

UMTANUM RIDGE

12

Yakima

Yakama
Indian
Reservation

Yakima R.

97

SADDLE MTS.

82

Columbia National
Wildlife Refuge

RATTLESNAKE
HILLS

Moses Lake

Potholes
Reservoir

Hanford Reach
National
Monument

Richland

82

12

Kennewick

Pasco

Snake R.

Pullman

395

90

1040

12

Walla Walla

Umatilla
National Forest

BLUE
MTS.

12

PACIFIC
OCEAN

N
W E
S

0   miles   100

Interstate

Major
Highway

City or Town

State Capital

Highest Point
in State

Mountains

Historic Site

National Forest

National Park

State Park

National Wildlife Refuge

Other Points of Interest

State Song

Washington My Home

words and music by Helen Davis

BOOKS

Carew-Miller, Anna. *Chief Seattle*. Broomall, PA: Mason Crest Publishers, 2002.

Downey, Tika. *Washington: The Evergreen State*. New York: Rosen Publishing, 2010.

Issacs, Sally. *Bill and Melinda Gates*. Mankato, MN: Heinemann-Raintree, 2009.

Riley, Gail Blasser. *Volcano! The 1980 Mount St. Helens Eruption*. New York: Bearport Publishing, 2006.

Smithyman, Kathryn. *Nations of the Northwest Coast*. New York: Crabtree Publishing, 2003.

WEBSITES

Official State of Washington Homepage:
www.access.wa.gov

The Washington State Historical Society:
www.wshs.org

The Washington State Senate Page Program:
www.leg.wa.gov/senate/administration/pageprogram/Pages/default.aspx

Steven Otfinoski has written more than ninety fiction and nonfiction books for young readers. His previous works for Marshall Cavendish include books on states, history, and animals. Otfinoski lives in Connecticut with his wife, a high school teacher and editor.

Tea Benduhn writes books and edits a magazine. She lives in the beautiful state of Wisconsin with her husband and two cats.

Page numbers in **boldface** are illustrations.

★ INDEX ★